Watch Me Grow!

A Down-to-Earth Look
at Growing Food in the City

Written by Deborah Hodge

Photographed by Brian Harris

Kids Can Press

For Finn and Jack, who love to eat ripe, red strawberries from their grandma's garden, and for Alexandra, a budding urban gardener. More blueberry pie for all of you! — DH

To Mother Earth, Father Sun and all the people who see the beauty and do the work! — BH

Acknowledgments

Thank you to FarmFolkCityFolk Society and photographer Brian Harris for contributing his lovely photographs to this book. A portion of Brian's royalties will be used to fund FarmFolkCityFolk's programs. FarmFolkCityFolk is a not-for-profit society working to cultivate a local, sustainable food system. Our projects provide access to, and protection of, food lands; support local, small-scale growers and producers; and engage communities in the celebration of local food. Please see www.farmfolkcityfolk.ca.

Thank you also to Emily Hodge for being an inspiring model of sustainable living and for showing us her wonderful ways of growing food with young children.

Finally, a sincere thank you to Valerie Wyatt and Sheila Barry, both excellent editors and keen urban gardeners, and to Julia Naimska for her beautiful design.

Text © 2011 Deborah Hodge
Photographs © 2011 Brian Harris

Kids Can Press acknowledges the financial support of the Government of Ontario, through the Ontario Media Development Corporation's Ontario Book Initiative; the Ontario Arts Council; the Canada Council for the Arts; and the Government of Canada, through the BPIDP, for our publishing activity.

Published in Canada by
Kids Can Press Ltd.
25 Dockside Drive
Toronto, ON M5A 0B5

Published in the U.S. by
Kids Can Press Ltd.
2250 Military Road
Tonawanda, NY 14150

www.kidscanpress.com

Edited by Valerie Wyatt
Designed by Julia Naimska

This book is smyth sewn casebound.
Manufactured in Singapore, in 10/2010
by Tien Wah Press (Pte) Ltd.

FSC
www.fsc.org
MIX
Paper from
responsible sources
FSC® C019704

CM 11 0 9 8 7 6 5 4 3 2 1

Library and Archives Canada Cataloguing in Publication

Hodge, Deborah
    Watch me grow! : a down-to-earth look at growing food in the city / written by Deborah Hodge ; photographs by Brian Harris.

ISBN 978-1-55453-618-4

1. Urban agriculture—Juvenile literature. I. Harris, Brian, 1951–
II. Title.

S494.5.U72H63 2011   j630.9173'2   C2010-904768-0

Kids Can Press is a *Corus*™ Entertainment company

GROWING
Page 4

SHARING
Page 12

In a bustling city, children and adults are growing delicious food for themselves and others to eat. As they tend their gardens, people are caring for nature, their neighborhoods and each other. They are sharing food and friendships and making the city a better place to live.

Would you like to explore the gardens in the city? Pull on your hat, grab a watering can and let's go!

EATING
Page 20

CARING
Page 28

GROWING

A seed is a new life, waiting to grow. It can sprout anywhere — even in a busy city!

All the seed needs is a soft bed of soil, a cool drink of water and the warm touch of the sun. Give it these things and, like magic, a tiny green shoot will push up out of the rich, dark earth.

In every corner of the city, green shoots are springing up and turning into fruits and vegetables. Gardeners everywhere are planting seeds and growing food.

As you wander through the city, look carefully. Where do you see food growing?

Here are some places to look: backyards, front yards, rooftops, boulevards, vacant lots, fire escapes, balconies, patios, windowsills and kitchen counters.

You can grow food almost anywhere that has soil, sunlight and water — even in some of the city's hidden or unusual spaces.

Do you have a patch of earth or container you can turn into a garden?

Some gardens are big. Others are small. You can grow food in any size of garden.

On a windowsill, you can plant sprouts or herbs. Tomatoes and lettuce grow well in pots on a balcony. Squash, cucumbers, watermelons and other large plants like to stretch out in a front or back yard. Along a narrow boulevard, there's space for towers of beans or tall stalks of corn.

Raspberries, peas and other vines are happy climbing up a fence. And on a rooftop, you can grow almost anything. How about radishes? Crunchy, red and peppery!

Growing a Herb Garden

A sunny windowsill is a great place to grow herbs such as basil, oregano or parsley. Put seeds or small plants into potting soil in flowerpots or a window box. Add water and watch them grow!

8

Bok, bok, bok ... Can you hear the chickens?

Some city people are growing animals for food, too. They keep chickens in their yards and eat the eggs they lay. The chickens run and scratch outdoors and produce eggs with bright orange yolks.

Honeybees in a rooftop garden or backyard hive make sweet honey — perfect on toast or in a fruit smoothie.

SHARING

In the city, people are sharing gardens and food.

Some gardeners share plots of land where they plant and harvest their food together.

Others grow extra fruits and vegetables to share with people who don't have enough to eat.

Still other people have garden space and little time or energy to use it. They pair up with people who want to garden but don't have land. At harvest time, the partners share the fruits and vegetables the garden produces.

How do you like to share?

These children are in a community garden — a piece of land that is tended by a group of people. The children work together to dig, plant, weed and water the garden.

Community gardens are good for neighborhoods. Neighbors of all ages and from many backgrounds get to know one another as they grow food side by side. Look for these shared gardens at community centers, parks, schools, apartment complexes or wherever people gather.

Community gardens offer a peaceful place in the midst of the traffic and hum of the city. They provide a home for birds, bees and other wild creatures. Best of all, they produce garden-fresh food!

Is there a community garden in your neighborhood?

Feeding Your Garden
When the soil is healthy, so is the food you grow. Add goodness to your garden by digging in compost — a well-rotted mixture of fruit and vegetable scraps, leaves, plant clippings and other garden waste. The soil needs food, too!

Lots of gardeners in the city grow food for themselves. But there are also farmers who grow food to sell. They sell what they grow at farmers' markets or to customers who buy a share of their crop for the year.

Many city farmers have their own plots of land. But some make an agreement with other people to farm their yards. The yard owners get some of the produce, while the farmer sells the rest. It's a new way to share.

Is there a city farmer near you?

Animals share our gardens, too! Soon these eggs will hatch, and there will be baby birds in the garden. Chirp, chirp ...

A city garden is a home for birds, butterflies, bees, squirrels, earthworms and many other wild creatures. The garden gives them food, shelter and a place to have their babies.

In return, the animals help the gardens. Birds eat garden pests, and earthworms help make the soil rich. Bees, butterflies and other insects spread pollen, the flower dust that helps fruits and vegetables produce new plants.

Many city gardeners plant flowers among their vegetable plants to attract these helpful insects. Some also place beehives in their yards. Bzz, bzz ...

Sharing Your Garden
Invite bees and other insects into your garden by growing big, bright sunflowers. Welcome birds by making them a bird-bath, birdhouse or feeder.

EATING

All across the city, children and grown-ups are eating food they have planted and harvested themselves.

Ripe, red strawberries, juicy watermelons and buttery corn on the cob. Leafy, green spinach, spicy peppers and tart, purple plums. Almost every kind of food you can imagine is growing in the city.

Families, friends and neighbors are gathering to cook and share meals. They know that eating together is a special thing to do.

Pass the blueberry pie, please!

You can grow food for dinner in any size of garden.

From a windowsill garden, you can pick herbs for a pasta sauce. Containers on a balcony can provide lettuce and radishes for a salad. And in a backyard or community garden, you can harvest vegetables for a soup or stew.

If you grow more food than you can eat in the summer, save some for winter meals. Freeze peas, beans, corn and other vegetables. Make crunchy pickles from cucumbers. Turn raspberries into jam and preserve peaches and other fruits by canning them.

Growing a Pizza Garden
Grow everything you need for a pizza dinner by planting your favorite veggies and herbs. How about tomatoes, garlic, spinach, zucchini, oregano and basil? Layer the chopped veggies on a pita, add some grated cheese and bake. Delicious!

These girls are having fun in a community kitchen — a kitchen space where people cook and eat together.

A community kitchen is a great place to cook food and make friends. The kitchen can be in a school, church, community center or any place there is room for people to gather and share food.

In some community kitchens, children cook with the food they grow. They use fruits, vegetables, herbs and even grains, such as rye, that they harvest from their gardens.

With the help of chefs, the children turn the food into breads, salads, soups, curries, stir-fries and many other yummy dishes.

What do you like to cook?

Sipping a Fruit Smoothie
Have fun in your own kitchen! Put ripe berries in a blender with yogurt, ice and milk. Sweeten to taste. Give it all a whir, pour into a glass and enjoy your refreshing drink.

24

Many city people want to eat healthy, fresh food, but not everyone can grow all the food they need, so they shop for it instead.

Some go to a farmers' market, where buyers mingle with farmers to buy food grown in their own area. Others go to grocery stores that offer local foods in season.

Still others buy food from city farmers who are growing crops and raising animals right in the city or on its edges.

The city is bursting with food. You can find it if you look.

Are you hungry? Let's eat!

CARING

These people are harvesting apples from the neighborhood trees. They will donate the fruit to community kitchens or food programs for hungry people.

Everywhere in the city, people are caring for their gardens and caring for each other.

They're sharing gardens, kitchens and food. They're learning about their neighbors and themselves. They're making the city a more beautiful place to live.

As their gardens grow, so do their friendships with one another.

There are many ways to care. Can you think of some?

Many city gardeners think about nature and the earth as they tend their gardens.

They know that everything that grows is connected in a big family of living things and that keeping the soil healthy keeps our food healthy. They also know that a garden is a special place for the wild creatures that share our city home.

When we garden, we are caring for nature and for the plants and animals of our world. As we watch seeds sprout and grow into plump fruits and vegetables, we are thankful for the soil, sun and rain that give life to our plants and all living things.

Best of all, we can harvest the bounty of our garden and eat fresh, tasty food we have grown ourselves!

What will you grow?

Caring for Our Future
When we grow our own food and keep the soil healthy, we are caring for ourselves, our cities and our future. Care for your garden and the earth by feeding the soil, using water wisely and respecting all living things.

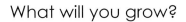

About This Book and Urban Agriculture

The city shown in this book is Vancouver, Canada — a beautiful, thriving, multicultural center that hugs the mountains and ocean. Like many cities of the world, Vancouver has embraced urban agriculture.

Urban agriculture is a rapidly expanding social movement that seeks to improve our cities. Gardens create green space and beauty. They provide a home for wildlife and keep us connected with nature. They encourage cooperation and community building. Most importantly, urban agriculture allows us to grow our own food and control how it's produced. Many urban gardeners use earth-friendly practices such as composting, mulching, seed saving, water conservation, natural fertilizers and pest management.

Gardening engages children in the act of growing and teaches them where their food comes from. Growing food is an inspirational and educational experience that every child can participate in.

Thank you to all the dedicated urban gardeners, farmers and sustainable living advocates who generously allowed us to write about them and photograph their work:

China Creek Community Garden
City Farm Boy
Cypress Community Gardens
Davie Village Community Garden
Emily Hodge, Jack Garner, Finn Garner and Alexandra Grove
Fresh Roots Urban CSA
Glen Valley Organic Farm Cooperative
Grant's Gourmet Gardens
Home Grow-in Grocer
Klipper's Organic Acres
Organic Acres — Granville Island Market
Project Chef
Providence Farm
Southlands Farms
Sprouting Chefs
Vancouver Convention Centre
Vancouver Farmers' Markets
Vancouver Fruit Tree Project
World in a Garden Project